UNVEILING VERSES

A COMPELLING COMPILATION ON LIFE

GAURI ADMUTHE AND HIMANI SHAH

We dedicate this book to our beloved parents, our cherished friends, and all the remarkable individuals who have touched our lives meaningfully. We're also thankful for those who gave us the worst and best memories. Your unwavering support, guidance, and presence have enriched our journey and inspired us to create this work. Thank you for being a part of our lives and sharing our joys and challenges.

Contents

Contents

Contents

Motivation

Contents

Contents

Life

1. The Dance of Existence

Life is a waltz, a delicate dance
Twirling through moments, taking a chance
Each step a rhythm, each breath a song
In the symphony of existence, we belong
We sway with the winds of change
Embracing the highs and lows, rearrange
Our perspectives, our hopes, our fears
Navigating the ebbs and flows, shifting gears
Through valleys of sorrow and peaks of joy
We find solace in the moments that deploy
Lessons learned, connections made
In the tapestry of life, our stories fade
But in the dance, we find our truth
Embracing the beauty of age and youth
For life is a journey, a fleeting glance
A dance of existence, a timeless romance.

2. Cradles of Innocence

In the cradle of innocence, so pure and mild,
Where every smile and coo is like a cherished rhyme,
Tiny fingers grasp the world, curious and beguiled,
A newborn's laughter echoes, a melody divine.
Soft whispers of lullabies, cradle's gentle sway,
Innocence blooming like flowers in early May,
In the embrace of love, a precious life's ballet.
Innocence's bliss, in each giggle and sigh,
A canvas of wonder, beneath the azure sky,
In the cradle of innocence, where dreams first fly.

3. Whispers of Wonder

Skipping through meadows, chasing dreams in flight,
Imagination's playground, where wonders never cease,
Laughter like bubbling streams, hearts pure and bright,
Childhood's magic dances, in moments of peace.
Sun-kissed days of play, dreams take to the skies,
Innocent hearts soaring, like birds that freely fly,
In the garden of innocence, where dreams never die.
Innocence's joy, in each sandcastle built,
A symphony of laughter, in moments unfelt,
Childhood's memories, in each heart forever quilt.

4. Turbulent Tides of Youth

Awash in emotions, a turbulent sea of change,
Where dreams take flight, yet doubts often reign,
Hearts flutter like butterflies, feelings rearrange,
In this labyrinth of discovery, where growth is gained.
Amidst the storms of youth, passions bloom and rise,
Dreams painted in hues, beneath the starlit skies,
Adolescence's dance, in a world of endless tries.
Dreams chased with fervour, in every daring leap,
A tapestry of experiences, in memories deep,
Adolescence's journey, in every secret keep.

5. Perceptions of Beauty

Why am I only half pretty?
Why do I appear different in videos than in person?
Why do my candid photos embarrass me?
Yet when I take them, I look just fine.
Why am I only pretty sometimes?
And why do I even care?
I tell others it doesn't matter,
But somehow, it seems to matter to everyone but me.

6. Insecurities In a Perfectly Imperfect Body

I know I have this body,
But oh, how I hate it so.
I can't help but feel flawed,
Each time I look in the mirror.
My height, a constant reminder,
Of my lack of stature and grace.
My legs, too thick and heavy,
Never fitting society's ideal space.
And these hips, so unproportional,
They bring me nothing but shame.
How I long for a different shape,
To escape from this never-ending game.
My hair, a tangled mess,
Never falling perfectly in place.
Without makeup on my face,
I feel invisible and less.
I hate it all, every inch,
Of this body that I possess.
But deep down I know,
These thoughts are not progress.

For hating oneself brings no good,
Only endless sorrow and pain.
So instead of loathing what I see,
I'll embrace myself with love again.

7. Invisible Beauty

Count your calories, a weight on the mind
I've never looked good in any jeans, a struggle to find
Wish I was like you, with the "perfect body" and the "ideal type"
In a world of standards, where beauty is ripe
Maybe I should just try harder, push through the pain
I'm no quick model, in a world so vain
If I get more pretty, will I finally fit in?
Do you think people will like me, with a new skin?
In the mirror, I see flaws and imperfections
Invisible beauty, lost in reflections
I long to be accepted, to feel desired
In a world of standards, where beauty is required.

8. Embracing Self-Compassion

Oh, how I hate the new me, a stranger in my skin
I'm so sick of myself, the turmoil within
The times I'm disappointed in myself, a heavy weight
Can't get a thing right, trapped in self-debate
I long for the days when confidence reigned
When self-doubt was silenced, when I felt unchained
But now I stumble, in the shadows of doubt
Lost in a maze of self-critique, a relentless bout.

9. Breaking Free from Expectations

She stands in the shadow of her parents' expectations,
A heavy burden that weighs upon her young shoulders.
Their voices echo in her mind, filled with high aspirations,
But the weight of their hopes and dreams only makes her bolder.
With every criticism, she feels her confidence crumble,
As she tries to meet expectations that seem impossible.
Her self-worth tied to grades, a constant uphill struggle,
Leaving no room for mistakes, her future seems infallible.
Slowly she learns to let go of their rigid standards,
And focuses instead on discovering her own passions.
For true happiness comes from fulfilling one's heart's desires,
Not from meeting others' expectations in calculated fashion.

10. A bad dream

A bad dream, a haunting sight

In the stillness of night, a chilling fright

Aren't dreams supposed to be relaxing, serene?

Why do mine turn dark, a twisted scene?

In the depths of slumber, where shadows creep

I find myself lost, in a nightmare so deep

Monsters lurk in the corners of my mind

Twisting reality, leaving me blind

I try to escape, to wake from this dread

But the nightmare holds me, filling me with dread

I scream in silence, trapped in my own head

A bad dream, a torment, a feeling of dread

I toss and turn, in the grip of fear

Hoping for morning, for the nightmare to clear

But the darkness lingers, the terror remains

A bad dream, a torment, a soul in chains

So I cling to the hope, that dawn will break

And the shadows will fade, the fear will shake

A bad dream, a reminder of the mind's power

To create its own hell, in the midnight hour.

11. Flames of Passion

With fire in their eyes, they face the world bold,
Ambitions soar high, fueled by passion's flame,
Adventures beckon, in tales yet untold,
Youth's vibrant spirit, forever unchained.
Dreams sculpted in courage, against the winds that blow,
Hearts ablaze with fervour, in life's grand tableau,
Youth's anthem echoes, in every new tomorrow.
Youth's legacy written, in each daring quest,
A symphony of passion, in every life's test,
Youth's essence captured, in hearts that never rest.

12. Resilient Blooms of Hope

In the garden of sorrow, blooms hope's sweet refrain,
Petals of resilience unfurl through the pain,
Each tear a diamond, glistening in the night,
Life's tapestry woven with threads of light,
Beauty emerges, phoenix-like, from the ashes' flight.
Whispers of wisdom dance on the wind's soft sigh,
Echoes of laughter amid the silent sky,
Stars alight, guiding the way through the dark,
Hearts find solace, like ships in a tranquil harbor,
In the beauty of life's resilient, enduring spark.
Through shattered dreams and tempests fierce and wild,
Strength arises, a warrior undefiled,
In the crucible of adversity, diamonds are born,
Each scar a testament, to resilience worn,
Beauty thrives, in the courage to transform.
Amidst the ruins, a melody softly sings,
Hope's gentle touch mending broken wings,
Life's canvas painted with hues of sorrow and grace,
Embracing the scars, each line a cherished trace,
Beauty shines brightest, in life's resilient embrace.

13. Journey of Responsiblities

Responsibilities weigh like burdens to bear,
Paths chosen with care, ambitions set in stone,
Love's tender whispers, moments so rare,
Adulthood's journey, a symphony of its own.
Challenges met with grace, in life's unfolding tale,
Dreams woven with patience, like threads that never fail,
Adulthood's legacy, in every step and trail.
Wisdom's whispers heard, in each decision made,
A symphony of life's notes, in each accolade,
Adulthood's essence, in each role well played.

14. Lost in Autopilot

If I'm being honest, I'm done with everything
Nothing excites me, nothing makes me happy anymore
Where is my career going, I have no idea
And my life is a mess, feeling so sore.
It feels as if my life is on autopilot mode
Drifting through days without a sense of direction.
Lost in a sea of monotony, a heavy load
Yearning for a spark, a new connection.
The passion that once fueled my drive
Now flickers dimly, barely alive
Dreams deferred, hopes cast aside
In the shadows of doubt, I hide.

15. Embracing Hope Amidst Despair

In the depths of despair, my soul feels torn,
Life's struggles and sorrows, heavy to be borne.
Yet in the chaos, a flicker of hope survives,
A beacon of light, where faith thrives.
Through trials and tribulations, I journey on,
Though the road is rough, my spirit's not gone.
With each setback, I rise with determination,
Believing in brighter days, a new revelation.

16. Wisdom's Tapestry

The rush of life slows, like a steady stream,
Wisdom blooms like flowers, in the garden of the soul,
Memories weave tapestries, of dreams and esteem,
Middle age's grace, a story to extol.
Reflections of journeys, in the mirror of time,
Life's canvas painted, with hues rich and prime,
Middle age's wisdom, in every rhythm and rhyme.
Dreams revisited, in the twilight's gentle glow,
A symphony of echoes, in moments that flow,
Middle age's legacy, in hearts that always know.

17. Mind's Maze

Lost in thoughts, a labyrinth of the mind
Wandering through corridors, seeking to find
The echoes of memories, the whispers of dreams
In the depths of thought, where reality teems
A maze of emotions, a tangle of fears
Lost in the labyrinth, shedding silent tears
The mind's twists and turns, a puzzle to solve
In the realm of thoughts, where mysteries evolve
Lost in contemplation, in a world of my own
Drifting through thoughts, in a realm unknown
The past and future intertwine, in a dance of time
In the labyrinth of the mind, where thoughts climb
So I wander through the corridors of my mind
Lost in thoughts, seeking what I may find
In the maze of emotions, in the depths of my soul
Lost in thoughts, yet feeling whole.

18. Echoes of Time

Wrinkles map journeys, etched with time's embrace,
Stories whispered softly, like autumn's gentle breeze,
Wisdom's crown shines, in lines on weathered face,
Elderhood's wisdom, a legacy that frees.
Echoes of laughter, in memories old and dear,
Life's chapters written, with joy and with tear,
Elderhood's embrace, in each moment sincere.
Legacy's whispers heard, in each passing day,
A symphony of life's songs, in twilight's sway,
Elderhood's essence, in hearts that forever stay.

19. Falling asleep

Falling asleep is peaceful, a gentle retreat
A moment of solace, a sweet, dreamy feat
In the quiet of night, as the world fades away
I find my sanctuary, where my worries stray
The soft lullaby of the night whispers in my ear
Guiding me gently, dispelling all fear
I drift into slumber, my mind finally at ease
Embracing the stillness, the calm, the release
In the realm of dreams, I find my respite
A place of magic, where my soul takes flight
Where troubles dissolve, and burdens are light
Falling asleep is peaceful, a gift in the night
So let me close my eyes, and surrender to rest
To the embrace of darkness, where I am truly blessed
For in the realm of dreams, I find my true self
Falling asleep is peaceful, it's where I find myself.

20. Whispers of the Unseen

A ghost, a haunting sight unseen

In the shadows of life, a chilling dream

Aren't souls supposed to be at rest?

Why do ghosts linger, a presence unblest?

In the quiet of night, their whispers sigh

Echoes of sorrow, a mournful cry

Lost in the realm between worlds unknown

A ghostly figure, a spirit alone

Their presence unnerving, a shiver down the spine

A specter of the past, a tale intertwined

With the living, they dance in the shadows

A haunting reminder of life's unknowns

Do they seek solace, or vengeance untold?

Their ethereal presence, a mystery to behold

A ghost, a soul in limbo, a spirit adrift

In the realm of the unseen, a spectral gift

So we listen to their whispers, their silent plea

For understanding, for empathy

A ghost, a haunting sight unseen

In the stillness of life, a chilling dream.

21. Ocean's Embrace

All alone in an ocean,
Feel my soul, pure devotion,
It's the only thing that takes my breath away.
All these waves, pull me under.
Lost in the vast expanse,
Embraced by the ocean's dance,
I surrender to its mighty power,
In this moment, I feel alive, not cower.
Beneath the surface, I find peace,
As the waves gently cease,
In the depths, I am free,
To be who I am, just me.
The ocean whispers secrets untold,
In its depths, my spirit unfolds,
I am one with the sea,
In its embrace, I am truly me.

22. Pages of Escape

Lost in a book, a world unfolds
Where stories dance and dreams are told
In the pages of escape, I find my retreat
A sanctuary of words, where reality meets
Characters come alive, in the depths of my mind
In the tapestry of tales, a treasure to find
Lost in the plot twists, the turns of fate
In the world of books, I navigate
Through adventures and mysteries, I roam
In the realms of fantasy, I find my home
Lost in the prose, the rhythm of rhyme
In the pages of escape, where time chimes
I lose myself in the words, in the magic they weave
In the power of storytelling, I believe
For in the world of books, I find solace and peace
In the pages of escape, where my soul finds release.

23. Royal Reflections

I'ma treat me like a queen,
In my own realm, I reign supreme,
Looking at you, got me thinking nonsense,
In your presence, my heart's defense.
I'm just chilling, I'm talking,
In my own world, I'm walking,
Through the echoes of my mind,
A royal spirit, I find.
With grace and poise, I stand tall,
In my own kingdom, I heed the call,
To honor myself, to cherish my worth,
A queen in my own right, since birth.
So I'll embrace my royal crown,
In my own castle, I won't back down,
For in my reflection, I see a queen,
A powerful force, serene and keen.

24. Nourishment of the Soul

*I don't understand why people need others to make them feel
alive,
For me, I think it's just food, a simple drive
Food doesn't speak, it doesn't irritate
It just simply makes us happy, a comforting state
In the flavors and aromas, a world unfolds
A symphony of tastes, a story untold
Food nourishes not just the body, but the soul
In its warmth and comfort, it makes us whole
From the first bite to the last, a journey begins
Through textures and spices, where joy wins
Food brings people together, in a shared delight
A feast for the senses, a culinary flight.*

25. Embracing the Journey

Life brings hardships no matter what
Even till the day comes to dawn
Through trials and tribulations, we must trot
In the darkness, a glimmer of hope is drawn
Challenges test our strength and will
But with perseverance, we can prevail
Each obstacle a chance to fulfill
Our potential, to rise and set sail
So let us face each hurdle with grace
Embracing the journey, come what may
For in the struggle, we find our place
And emerge stronger, day by day.

26. A Yearning for Simplicity

I yearn for a life of simplicity,
Where the raindrops fall with grace,
And the clouds calmly drift above,
In my small and humble space.
Whether by the shore or mountain high,
I seek contentment in every view.
For it's in nature where I find solace,
In a life that's pure and true.
New roads, new cities, new horizons,
Do not entice me, I confess.
For all I desire is a heart full of joy,
With no worries of worldly stress.
No race to run for money or fame,
No holes to fill with endless strife.
My only goal is to embrace simplicity,
And live a simple, peaceful life.
So let me edit this poem anew,
To capture my desires just right.
For all I truly want is simplicity,
A humble haven from dawn till night.

27. Seaside Symphony

Upon the sands where whispers weave,
A symphony of waves beneath,
The ocean's breath, a timeless rhyme,
In every crest, a tale of time.
The sun, a painter's brush in hand,
Strokes of gold on azure land,
Where seagulls dance in graceful flight,
Their cries blend with the fading light.
Footprints etched in sandy shores,
Memories born, then swept ashore,
The beach, a canvas vast and free,
Where dreams and tides forever meet.
In shells, secrets softly sigh,
Echoes of a distant sky,
And as the stars their vigil keep,
The beach whispers secrets deep.
So, listen close to nature's song,
Where ocean's melody belongs,
For in the beach's timeless view,
Lies the peace that's ever true.

28. Screened Escape

She sits in silence, eyes transfixed,
Lost in worlds on screens affixed,
A flickering dance of light and sound,
Where troubles fade, and peace is found.
Remote in hand, she switches scenes,
From sitcom laughs to drama's schemes,
A marathon of shows to hide,
The storm that rages deep inside.
Each episode, a fleeting respite,
From battles fought in day's harsh light,
Characters' lives become her own,
A temporary refuge known.
But as the credits start to roll,
Reality's weight begins to toll,
Her problems, paused but not erased,
Awaiting in the quiet space.
Yet still, she seeks the screen's embrace,
A fleeting escape, a hiding place,
For in the glow of TV's glow,
Her fears and worries seem to slow.
But deep within, a whisper grows,
That true solace lies in what she knows,

Facing demons, embracing strife,
Is the journey to reclaim her life.

29. Earthly Beings

Oh, how the people on Earth are made
From stardust and dreams, in a cosmic parade
Each one unique, a story to tell
In this vast universe, where we all dwell
Oh, how the people on Earth live
In cities and forests, in valleys and hills
Seeking connection, seeking their place
Navigating life's intricate maze
Oh, how the people on Earth love
With hearts full of passion, with souls intertwined
Embracing the joy, weathering the storm
In this grand tapestry, where we are born
Oh, Earthly beings, so diverse and grand
May we cherish each other, hand in hand
For in this world of wonder and strife
It is love that sustains us, the essence of life.

30. Mountains

Mountains stand tall, ancient wise
Carved by time and nature
Their peaks touch the sky
Silent sentinels of the land
Majestic and grand, they command respect
Their slopes cloaked in green and white
Eternal witnesses to the passage of time
A sanctuary for creatures day and night
Mountains, stoic and unyielding
Yet filled with a quiet grace
A reminder of life's enduring strength
And the beauty of nature's embrace
So stand in awe of these giants of earth
Marvel at their rugged splendor
For in their presence, we find solace
And a sense of peace so tender.

31. Trees

In the forest's embrace, the trees stand tall,
Their branches reaching for the endless top,
Roots buried deep, connecting one and all,
A symphony of whispers as winds growl.
Majestic guardians of the earth,
Their leaves rustling in the gentle breeze,
Each one a monument to rebirth,
A sanctuary for birds and bees.
In their sturdy trunks, stories are told,
Of ancient wisdom and secrets untold,
Their presence a comfort, a sight to behold,
In their shade, the weary find solace untold.
Oh, how we owe our thanks to thee,
Oh, noble trees, so grand and free,
For in your shelter, we find peace,
In your beauty, our souls release.

32. Elements of Earth

In the vast expanse of sandy soil and water,
The elements dance in harmonious flow,
Whispers of ancient stories explained by the wind,
As the grains of sand shift and glow.
Beneath the surface lies a world unseen,
Where roots entwine and life begins to grow,
Drawing sustenance from the earth and sky,
In a symphony of colors that ebb and flow.
Water trickles through the grains of sand,
Nourishing the earth with its gentle touch,
Creating life where once there was none,
A testament to nature's power and such.
In this landscape of sand, soil, and water,
We find a beauty that is timeless and true,
A reminder of the cycles of life and death,
And the infinite possibilities that ensue.
So let us cherish this sacred union,
Of sand, soil, and water intertwined,
And remember the beauty that surrounds us,
In this world that is endlessly kind.

Love And Friendship

33. The Fear of Attachment

Socializing is very rare for me
Or maybe it's just rare because I get attached too quickly.
But lucky you, I guess, not so lucky for me
Because you don't like me, if anything you'd probably ditch me.
The fear of attachment grips my heart
A vulnerability I try to shield.
But in my eagerness to connect, to impart
I often find myself left in the field.
You, with your walls up high
Unwilling to let anyone in
I reach out, hoping to defy
The odds, but it's a battle I can't win.
But despite the risks, I still try
To forge connections, to break free.
From the fear that makes me shy
Hoping one day, someone will see.
That beneath the fear of attachment
Lies a heart that longs to connect.
To find a bond that's meant to match
A friendship that's true and perfect.

34. Friendship's Healing Embrace

In the shadow of loss, a hand reaches out to guide,
A friend's embrace, in sorrow's tide, a solace by my side.
Though one departed, leaving wounds unseen,
Another's touch, a healing stream, where hope begins to glean.
Together we walk, through trials and fears,
Their presence, a balm, to dry my tears.
In friendship's bond, a strength revealed,
When love departs, a friend's hand shields.

35. Embers of Friendship

In friendship's gentle glow, we find our light,
A beacon strong to guide us through the night.
Through valleys low and mountains high we stride,
With steadfast hearts, side by side.
In laughter shared, our spirits rise,
As wings of joy take flight into the skies.
With every word, a spark ignites anew,
Fueling dreams and goals we pursue.
When shadows loom and doubts assail,
A friend's encouragement will never fail.
With gentle words and unwavering support,
We find the strength to press on, never abort.
For in the bond of true companionship,
We find the fuel for our soul's fellowship.
Together we weather life's storms and strife,
Fueled by friendship, igniting life.

36. Threads of Friendship

In the tapestry of time, you've been my constant thread,
Through laughter and tears, you've been my rock, my stead.
From playground adventures to late-night talks,
You've been my confidante, my partner in walks.
In the tapestry of life, you shine like a star,
Guiding me through darkness, no matter how far.
Your presence is a gift, a treasure so rare,
In your friendship, I find solace, beyond compare.
Through the seasons of change, we've grown side by side,
Our bond unbreakable, with love as our guide.
In the symphony of memories, you're the melody sweet,
Forever grateful for the friendship we keep.

37. So-called Mates

In a whirlwind of laughter and smiles, she found her place
Amongst the friends, she thought would understand her soul
But as the days passed, the facade began to fade
And she felt the weight of their expectations take their toll
She tried to mold herself to fit their mold
But each shape she took left her feeling more alone
Lost in a sea of laughter and inside jokes
She longed to find a space that truly felt like home
The girl who once felt like she belonged
Now wanders through the shadows of their camaraderie
Searching for a glimmer of herself in their midst
But finding only echoes of what she used to be
Her heart aches for the freedom to be true
To stand out from the crowd and shine her light
But in the company of those who cannot see
She struggles to find her way through the night.

38. Call me anytime

When I say, "Call me anytime"
What I mean is, I'll be there
No matter the hour, no matter the weather
In your joy, in your despair
I don't care if it's 2 in the morning
Or if the rain is pouring down
If you've just had an argument
Or if you're feeling like you'll drown
Even if you're miles away
I'll bridge the distance with my heart
In the darkness of night or the light of day
I'll listen, I'll care, I'll play my part
So when I say, "Call me anytime"
Know that my words are sincere
I'll be your rock, your shelter, your guide
In your journey, I'll always be near.

39. Bound by Love

You give me strength and hope,
And you just need to know,
I love you.
Oh, how deep friendships can go.
In your presence, I find solace,
In your words, I find grace,
Your love lifts me up,
In your embrace, I find my place.
Through laughter and tears,
Through the passing years,
Our bond grows stronger,
Our friendship lasts longer.
In the depths of my heart,
You hold a special part,
A friend so true and dear,
In your love, I have no fear.
Together we stand, hand in hand,
Bound by love, we understand,
The power of a friendship so true,
Forever grateful for you.

40. Heartstrings Entwined

In the dance of life, where paths entwine,
Love and friendship, a tapestry divine,
Two souls bound by fate's intricate design,
In the symphony of hearts, forever aligned.
Through laughter's echo and tears that fall,
In the embrace of friendship's gentle call,
Love's melody sings, a harmonious thrall,
As bonds of affection stand strong and tall.
Hand in hand, through joys and fears,
Shared dreams sparkle like crystal-clear spheres,
In the warmth of love, wiping away tears,
Friendship's beacon, through the passing years.
Hearts beat as one in a rhythm so sweet,
Love's symphony, a timeless feat,
Friendship's embrace, a sanctuary complete,
In this journey of souls, love and friendship meet.

41. Whispers of the Heart

In the garden of friendship, a bond so true
A girl's heart beats for a friend she knew
But the winds of change, a subtle breeze
Carry whispers of longing, hidden with ease
Amidst the laughter and shared delight
A girl's feelings bloom in the moon's soft light
Yet the one she cherishes, set to depart
Leaves her heart aching, torn apart
In the shadows of secrets, her love resides
A silent yearning, where her heart confides
But the one she treasures, set to move on
Leaves her dreams shattered, her hopes withdrawn
In the quiet of night, her heart's refrain
Echoes softly, a bittersweet pain
A love unspoken, a bond untold
In the depths of her soul, a tale unfolds.

42. Tethered to You

I was hanging out with you, in moments so true
And then I realized, in a sudden view
That I'm only alive around you, in your presence so bright
I didn't wanna believe that you are my reason for everything, my guiding light
I didn't wanna believe that I could lose you, my heart in fear
But I can't help it, you've become my reason, my anchor so dear
And I can't quit it, this feeling so strong
Cause I'm stuck on you, in your love I belong.

43. Seeds of Redemption

In the garden of our love, I plant my words,
Each petal a confession, each thorn a regret.
For I have not been the gentle rain,
Nurturing the roots of our love's domain.
Instead, I've been the tempest, wild and free,
Unleashing storms that shook our unity.
I'm sorry for the lightning in my temper's fray,
For the clouds that obscured our sunny day.
I've been the winter's chill,
Frosting over moments meant to thrill.
I should have been the summer's warm embrace,
Melting walls of ice with love's grace.
But in this garden, I offer a seed,
A promise of growth, of love's true creed.
I'll tend to it with patience and care,
For our love to blossom, beyond compare.

44. Hold Me Close

Don't you cry now,

What's the time now?

Time for goodbye,

Hold me, in your arms,

Just like you do.

Let the tears fall, let them flow,

But remember, I won't go.

In your heart, I'll always stay,

Even as we part our ways.

Hold me close, don't let me go,

In your love, I'll always know.

Though we say goodbye for now,

Our bond will endure, this I vow.

45. Heart's Deception

In the mirror's gaze, I question my heart,

Is it love or just a fleeting spark?

I admire your smile, your eyes so bright,

But is it love that keeps me up at night?

I convince myself it's just a ephemeral attraction,

A fleeting moment, a passing hush.

It's admiration for your charm and grace,

Not love's embrace, a different space.

Yet, in the silence of my mind,

Your presence lingers, undefined.

Is it lust that stirs my desire,

Or a deeper longing, a hidden fire?

I wrestle with these thoughts each day,

Trying to push love's whispers away.

But deep down, I know the truth,

My feelings for you, uncaged and uncouth.

So I dance in this delicate balance,

For now, I'll call it admiration's art,

But my heart knows, it's love's gentle start.

46. Whispers of Moonlight Love

Admiring you from afar,
As moonlight caresses your form,
The way your dress, a whispering silk,
Enchants the night with its charm.
Your eyes, like stars in a midnight sky,
Seeking a connection yet untold,
A dance of longing, a silent plea,
In every glance, a story unfolds.
His hands, like gentle breezes,
Through your hair they softly glide,
In every touch, a fleeting moment,
A symphony of passion, deep and wide.
But in this quiet ache of yearning,
I find a melody, sweet and keen,
For love's essence, beyond the physical,
Resides in dreams, pure and serene.
In shadows cast by love's soft glow,
I embrace this truth, serene and bold,
For in the unseen, love's truest form,
Is a treasure, more precious than gold.

47. Unspoken Thoughts

In the quiet corners of her mind, she lingers
The girl left in thoughts of unspoken yearning
Her heart aches with the weight of unanswered questions
Why couldn't they see the love she was offering?
She replays their moments together, searching for a sign
A glimmer of hope that he felt the same way
But instead, she finds herself lost in a maze of uncertainty
Wondering why she wasn't the one they chose to stay
Was she not enough, not beautiful or smart enough
To capture their wandering heart and hold it close
Or was it simply a twist of fate that led them away
Leaving her alone in the shadows of her own prose
So she stands on the edge of her own broken dreams
A girl left in thoughts of a love that could never be
But in her heart, she knows that she is strong enough
To carry on, to rise above, to set her spirit free.

48. Buried Feelings

In the quiet corners of her heart,
She hides a secret so profound,
A love that blooms in shadows dark,
Yet dares not make a sound.
Her laughter rings, her smiles bright,
But in her eyes, a hidden flame,
For her best friend, a guiding light,
Yet she pretends it's just a game.
She buries feelings deep within,
Concealed beneath a mask so true,
A friendship pure, a love unspoken,
A bond that only she and he knew.
Their laughter echoes in the night,
Their secrets shared beneath the stars,
But she keeps her love out of sight,
Afraid to break what they hold dear.
So she plays her part, the friend so kind,
While love wells up within her chest,
A silent ache, a bittersweet reminder,
Of the love she never will confess.
But in the quiet of the night,
When darkness cloaks her in its embrace,

She whispers softly to the moon,
Her love for him, a hidden grace.
And though the world may never know,
The depths of love within her heart,
She finds solace in their friendship,
And keeps her love a work of art.

49. Labyrinth of Apologies

In the labyrinth of our love, I weave my song,
Each note a twist, each melody a wrong.
For I've been the riddle, unsolved and strange,
A puzzle of contradictions, a pattern to rearrange.
Apologies echo through the maze of my heart,
Where shadows dance, and mysteries start.
I should have been the clear sky, not the fog,
Navigating through uncertainties like a rogue.
For moments lost in the moon's eclipse,
Casting shadows over our tender eclipse.
I should have been the stars, guiding and bright,
Leading us through the darkness of the night.
But in this labyrinth, I offer a key,
A symbol of unlocking what's meant to be.
I'll unravel the mysteries, untangle the knots,
So our love can flourish in bizarre plots.

50. Envy's Embrace

Jealousy, a bitter seed takes root
I wanna throw myself away, a heart in pursuit
All I see are girls, with perfect white-teeth
And perfect bodies, a standard out of reach
Their smiles gleam, like polished pearls
Their bodies sculpted, like precious curls
I compare and despair, in the mirror's cruel gaze
Envy's grip tightens, in a suffocating haze
I long to escape this cycle of self-doubt
To break free from jealousy's toxic bout
For beauty lies not in perfection's guise
But in the soul's light, that never dies.

51. One Person

Lost the chance to speak, lost the chance to trust
Lost the chance to love, turned to dust.
Who knew that one person could destroy
A weapon deployed, leaving me devoid of joy.
In the silence of betrayal, my voice silenced
In the shadows of doubt, my trust defied.
In the emptiness of heartbreak, my love denied
By one person's actions, my world capsized.
Their words like daggers, their actions like poison
One person's betrayal, my heart frozen.
In the aftermath of their deceit
I'm left alone, feeling incomplete.
But in the darkness, a flicker of light
A chance to rise, to reclaim my might
For though one person may cause pain
I will not let their actions be in vain.

52. Broken Trust

I lost trust in people, a heavy burden to bear
Their deceitful ways left me in despair
My heart shattered, my spirit crumbled
Betrayed by those in whom I humbly stumbled
Their lies and deceit made my life tremble
In the darkness of betrayal, I felt so humble
Pieces of my trust scattered, disassembled
Left to pick up the fragments, feeling so troubled
But in the wreckage, a glimmer of light
A chance to rebuild, to set things right
For in the brokenness, there lies a chance
To heal, to grow, to learn to dance.

53. Unwanted Echoes

I am never anything more
Than the one someone "didn't" need
The "taken advantage of" or the "used girl".
They left me
And I can't undo it.
Know me and you'll see why they left me.
Know me and you'll be able to see through pain
Know me and you'll find what was used
Know me and you'll find the one to choose.
After all the damage of them walking away,
I think I'll forever be the unwanted one.

54. Unseen Affections

I was nothing but an "extra" to you,
Easily discarded, deemed expendable,
Yet to me, you were all that I was,
My love, my desire, my care.
And yet, you were my friend,
Just because I was there.

55. Shattered Serenade

In the shadows of my heart, you dwell,
A bittersweet melody, a haunting spell.
Each day you break me, tear me apart,
Yet I can't deny the warmth of your art.
Your words cut deep, like a sharp knife,
Yet in your presence, I find solace, a rife.
The pain you bring, a familiar sting,
Yet in your eyes, a love so captivating.
I try to resist, to break free,
But your allure, a relentless plea.
You're the ache I can't erase,
The addiction I can't replace.
So I dance in this paradox, this endless game,
Where love and pain intertwine, without shame.
For you, the one who breaks me whole,
I'll keep loving, with a shattered soul.

56. Echoes of Regret

In the quiet of night, guilt softly creeps,
For not embracing love's sign, it weeps.
The grandest symbol, so pure and true,
Yet my heart chose paths anew.
In hindsight's gaze, regrets do swell,
Why didn't I, its allure, quell?
For kindness bloomed in every deed,
But my heart sought a different need.
The guilt of not reciprocating,
A love so genuine, everlasting.
But love's choice is a mystery untold,
In the heart's depths, its secrets hold.
Forgive my heart, for wandering far,
In search of love, like a distant star.
Your essence graces another's soul,
Completing their life, making it whole.

57. Unspoken Longing

In the quiet corners of her soul, she holds a secret wish,
To release the weight of expectations, to let go and relish,
The bond they share, deep and true,
But her heart aches for more, what can she do?
She yearns to free herself from the chains of desire,
To quell the longing, to extinguish the fire,
That burns within her, a silent plea,
To find contentment in what will be.
She knows she must surrender, to release the hold,
To cherish the connection, pure and bold,
To stop expecting, to set herself free,
And embrace the beauty of uncertainty.
For in the silence, true peace will reside,
Even if her heart longs for what's denied,
She must find solace in the love they share,
And let go of expectations, without a care.

58. Heartbreak

In the depths of sorrow, hearts do break apart,
A love once cherished now torn at the seams,
As shattered dreams lay heavy on the heart,
The pain of loss consumes in haunting streams.
Each beat a reminder of what once was,
Now lost in echoes of a love gone by,
A shadowed memory, a bitter cause,
Leaving behind tears that never dry.
Yet in this darkness, hope begins to bloom,
For healing whispers softly in the night,
A chance for hearts to mend and love resume,
To find new paths bathed in a hopeful light.
Though heartbreak may be large, in time it fades,
As love's sweet song in harmony cascades.

59. Echoes of Resilience

In the echo of memories, whispers of love once sown,
You were my everything, now in solitude I'm thrown.
Your absence like a void, a heartache so profound,
In the silence of nights, your absence resounds.
Yet I'll gather strength, mend what's torn and frayed,
For in the depths of resilience, I find a brighter day.
Alone, yet not defeated, from pain, I'll rise and grow,
For in letting go, I reclaim what I've come to know.

60. Silent Resonance of Betrayal

In shadows of the past, your presence lingers,
A ghostly whisper, a memory that stings.
Once a flame that warmed my soul's core,
Now ashes scattered, love's song no more.
You were the architect of my heart's design,
But your touch turned cruel, a venomous wine.
Promises woven in threads of deceit,
Now unravel, leaving scars that won't retreat.
You walked away, leaving shattered glass,
A mosaic of pain, a love that couldn't last.
Yet here you stand, with a mask so bright,
Pretending like it never happened, out of sight.
But I feel the echoes of your betrayal,
A silent scream, a lingering travail.
For wounds may heal, but scars remain,
A testament to love's bittersweet refrain.
So go on, with your charade and masquerade,
But know this truth can't be unmade.
You broke my heart, yet I stand tall,
Stronger now, for I've survived it all.

61. Infinite Hearts Aligned

In the vast expanse where souls entwine,
No heart beats for me like yours, divine.
In all the world's embrace, no love so true,
As the love I hold, solely for you.
Through oceans of time, our spirits entwined,
A bond so deep, in destiny designed.
No love compares to the flame we ignite,
Burning bright, in passion's tender light.
In every whisper of the wind's soft caress,
In every star that adorns night's dress,
Our love's melody, a timeless refrain,
In all the world, it shall forever reign.
No heart resonates with mine, this I swear,
In the tapestry of life, our love, rare.
In all the world's vast, boundless sea,
No love like yours, and none like mine, shall be.

62. In Search of Redemption

Search the definition of shame,

And I'm sure I'll be there, bearing the blame

Who's gonna save me now, from this dark place?

I hope it's you, with your love and grace

Don't change a thing, you're amazing, you say

In your eyes, I find a glimmer of light, a new way

In the depths of my despair, you offer a hand

Guiding me through the shadows, helping me stand

I carry the weight of my mistakes, my regrets

In the search for redemption, where forgiveness sets

I long to break free from the chains of shame

To find solace in your love, to reclaim my name

In your kindness, I see a path to healing

In your acceptance, I find a new beginning

For in your eyes, I see hope and redemption

In the journey of forgiveness, a soul's ascension.

63. Wings of Love

In the garden of life, two trees stand tall,
Their roots intertwined, a bond beyond the fall.
Their leaves whisper tales of love's endless quest,
A journey of hearts, where dreams find rest.
From their branches, I glean my wings,
Guided by their love, where hope sings.
Their smiles, like sunbeams on a cloudy day,
Illuminate my path, in every possible way.
Their dreams become mine, a sacred legacy,
Their joy, my compass, in life's vast sea.
For in making them happy, I find my true worth,
A journey of love, from the day of my birth.
Their love is my anchor, their pride my sail,
In their eyes, I find the strength to prevail.
For the greatest joy, in life's grand scheme,
Is to see their happiness, like a cherished dream.
So I spread my wings, with love as my guide,
In their embrace, I'll forever abide.
For their happiness is my eternal flame,
In their love, I find my name.

64. Love's Paradox: From Hurt to Endless Glee

In love's intricate dance, a paradox is found,
Where pain and affection intermingle, unbound.
For when love's depths are bravely explored,
Hurts transform into love, beautifully restored.
The heart's resilience, a remarkable sight,
Turning wounds into stars, shining bright.
With every ache, a new depth of care,
A testament to love's enduring affair.
Through tears and laughter, love's symphony plays,
Each note a reminder of love's timeless ways.
For in loving deeply, there's a magic untold,
Where hurt dissolves, and love's story unfolds.
So let love be fearless, let it dare to bleed,
For in its wounds, lies love's eternal seed.
And in loving until it hurts, we find the key,
To a world where hurt transforms into endless glee.

Motivation

65. Embrace of the Outcast

Don't kill me, I'm just a freak
A soul misunderstood, in shadows bleak
I'ma run away, on my own
Seeking solace, a place to be shown
Away from everyone else, in solitude's embrace
I'll find my refuge, in a hidden space
Cuz, I'm just a freak, a misfit soul
Yearning for acceptance, to feel whole
In the shadows of society, I find my light
Embracing my uniqueness, in the quiet of night
Don't judge me for who I am, for what I seek
For in my difference, a beauty unique
I'll carve my path, in the wilderness unknown
A wanderer, a dreamer, in a world of my own
Don't kill me, for I'm just a freak
In the embrace of the outcast, I find my peak.

66. Self-Love

Self-love, a virtue rare and true,
A treasure trove of beauty, shining through within.
In the mirror's gaze, I see a face,
Soft and gentle, full of grace.
The world may judge, the world may frown,
But I know my worth, I wear it proud.
My self-love shines like a crown,
A jewel in the heavens, with loud and proud.
Self-love is a journey, long and winding,
But with each step, I am refinding.
My strength, my courage, my heart,
All growing strong, a brand new start.
So let the world criticize and frown,
I'll keep on shining, never backing down.
For I am beautiful, I am strong,
And my self-love will never be wrong.

67. Time to Shine

Don't you cry now,
What's the time now?
It's time to rise, to spread your wings,
To chase your dreams, to do great things.
Don't let the tears cloud your sight,
The world is waiting, shining bright.
Embrace the moment, seize the day,
Let your spirit lead the way.
Time is fleeting, don't delay,
Make each second count, come what may.
With courage and strength, you'll find your way,
To a brighter tomorrow, a brand new day.

68. Flames of Resilient Passion

In the heart of every dream, a spark ignites,
Fierce flames of passion, reaching dizzying heights.
Fuelled by desire, relentless and bold,
Fire within, a story waiting to unfold.
Through trials and challenges, it blazes bright,
A beacon of hope, guiding through the night.
In every setback, it fuels resilience anew,
A blazing inferno, unstoppable and true.

69. Phoenix's Flight: A Symphony of Resilience

In every storm, behold the phoenix's flight,
Rising from ashes, a beacon of light.
With wings of courage, it soars above,
A symbol of resilience, unwavering love.
In the labyrinth of dreams, a golden thread,
Guiding the lost to where paths diverged and spread.
Through shadows of doubt, a lantern's glow,
Revealing truths only seekers know.
Like the lotus, bloom in muddy waters deep,
Embracing imperfections, treasures to keep.
Each scar a story, etched in time,
A map of victories, a rhythm, a rhyme.
In the symphony of life, find your unique note,
Harmonizing with the universe, a melody remote.
For in your essence, a universe resides,
A tapestry of stars, where destinies collide.

70. Courageous Flight of the Soul

In the symphony of life's highs and lows,
Where courage meets uncertainty's throes,
A flame within, unyielding, glows,
Igniting dreams that fiercely grow.
When shadows loom and doubts entwine,
Know your spirit, a star will shine,
Through storms and tests, your path define,
With resilience as your sacred sign.
Embrace the journey, face the fears,
Forge ahead through trials and tears,
Each setback a lesson, wisdom nears,
As your determination clears.
Rise above, let wings expand,
In the sky of dreams, take your stand,
Believe in yourself, with heart so grand,
And reach for stars, with outstretched hand.
Soar, oh soul, in skies aglow,
Let passion's fire within you flow,
For greatness waits, and dreams bestow,
The courage to conquer, to thrive, to grow.

71. Flames of Courage

In the darkness of night's stormy grip,
Where doubts and shadows start to slip. But in this chaos, a light
inside me burns,
A strong determination, my spirit yearns. Through thunder's roar
and lightning's flash,
I stand firm, unyielding to the crash. In chaos, resilience is born
anew,
With each sunrise, I rediscover what is true. In the storm's
symphony, I find my own tune,
Melody of courage that's makes me bloom.

72. Courageous Voyage: Navigating Life's Turbulent Seas

Upon tumultuous waters, the sea's tumultuous embrace,
Where tempests brew and fear finds its place.
Yet upon the billowing waves, a vessel defiantly sails,
A resolute heart, where courage never fails.
Through tumultuous swells and roaring gales' might,
I navigate, guided by perseverance's guiding light.
For on the distant horizon, destiny's call resounds,
And with each tempest weathered, resilience astounds.
In the vast expanse of ocean, my spirit roams free,
A sailor of dreams, embracing life's stormy sea.

73. Phoenix's Triumph: Rising from Adversity

In the midst of a blazing fire, chaos abounds,
But courage stands strong, never slowing down.
Within the heat's intense embrace, a spark ignites,
A strong desire to rise above life's darkest nights.
Through challenges and fiery trials,
I press on,
Fueled by determination, my spirit shines like the dawn.
In the crucible of adversity, strength is born anew,
Triumph emerges boldly, as challenges I pursue.
In the midst of flames, my spirit takes flight,
Like a phoenix rising from ashes soaring to new height.

74. Beacon of Courage: Rising from the Abyss

Within the depths' unfathomable expanse, shadows' realm,
Where uncertainties thrive and doubts overwhelm.
Yet within the abyss' obsidian embrace, a beacon shines,
A tenacious spirit, where fortitude entwines.
Through darkest depths and fears' haunting guise,
I ascend, fueled by courage's resolute rise.
For within the abyss' enigmatic embrace, truth prevails,
And from adversity's abyss, strength eternally avails.
In the abyss' silent echoes, my resolve reverberates,
A conqueror of fears, where courage dominates.

75. Guided by Resolve: Navigating Life's Labyrinth

In a maze of choices and twists, I seek clarity,
With determination, I navigate uncertaninty.
Each step reveals new insights, a revelation,
Resilience guides me through life's complication.
Illuminated by resolve, doubts fade away,
In this intricate dance, I find my way.
Through elusive bends and dead ends, I persist,
In the labyrinth of life, resilience is my gist.

76. Breaking the Chains of Comparison

Comparison is killing me, a relentless foe
I think I think too much, in a never-ending flow
About people who don't know me, their lives a mystery
I'm so sick of myself, trapped in this cycle of misery
I measure my worth against others' success
In a constant battle, a relentless stress
Their achievements shine bright, casting shadows on my own
I lose sight of my path, in comparison's cruel tone
I long to break free from this self-imposed cage
To silence the voices that fuel my rage
For I am unique, with a story to tell
Comparison's grip, a prison cell.

77. Wisdom in Time

The older I get, the more I see
How the world works, its complexity
No one's a hero, they're just like me
Navigating life's twists, trying to be free
Loving is hard, not all win
Heartaches and struggles, where to begin
But in growing older, wisdom unfolds
Lessons learned, stories untold
The mirror reflects the passage of time
Lines and wrinkles, a silent chime
Yet within, a depth of understanding
A richness of experience, life's branding
The older I get, the more I know
The highs and lows, the ebb and flow
In the tapestry of life, each thread weaves
A story of growth, of learning to believe.

78. Summit of Resolve

A towering peak, its summit shrouded in veils,
A daunting ascent where perseverance prevails.
With each sinew straining against gravity's decree,
I ascend with purpose, towards boundless majesty.
The zenith beckons, a distant celestial gleam,
I press forward, driven by an unyielding dream.
For atop the pinnacle, where skies and earth unite,
I shall grasp the ethereal, in triumphant flight.
Amidst rocks and echoes, my footsteps resound,
A testament to determination, profound and profound.

79. From Survivor to Inspirer

You've been through storms that few can bear
Suffered pain that seemed too much to bear
Yet here you stand, with steadfast light
For your trauma made you stronger, in its own right.
Through the darkness and the tears
You faced your fears, year after year
And though it scarred you deep within
It also molded you, made you tough as iron.
It takes true strength to face such pain
To fight against demons that try to restrain
But you refused to be a victim of your past
Instead, you emerged as a survivor at last.
And now as others struggle through their own storm
You can offer them hope and help them transform
For your experiences have given you wings to fly
And inspire others to never give up, even when they cry.

80. Unspoken Shame

You never talk about me to your friends,
In silence, our bond bends
Because you must be so embarrassed, I feel the weight
I dropped my grades in school, sealing my fate
The disappointment in your eyes, a silent reproach
I feel the shame, the unspoken approach
I let you down, my failures laid bare
In the shadows of inadequacy, I despair
I see the distance growing, the gap widening
As my mistakes echo, my shortcomings binding
I wish I could turn back time, rewrite the script
But the past lingers, a heavy crypt
I long for your pride, your words of support
But in my silence, I fall short
I'll work to regain your trust, to rise above
To mend the broken bond, to find love
You never talk about me to your friends
But in my heart, the message sends
I'll strive to make you proud, to erase the shame
To rebuild our connection, in a new flame.

81. Forgive Me, Mom and Dad

I'm sorry mom and dad,

For messing up my life, feeling so sad

I should've done better, made you proud

But I stumbled and fell, lost in the crowd

In 2009, you gave birth to me

Sweet little baby girl, full of glee

All were so happy, with hopes so high

But along the way, I lost my sky

I strayed from the path, made mistakes

Causing you heartache, my heart breaks

I wish I could turn back time, make things right

To undo the wrongs, to see the light

I know I've let you down, caused you pain

But please believe me, I'm not the same

I'm sorry mom and dad, for the tears I've shed

Forgive me, for I'm trying to mend

I'll work hard to make amends, to find my way

To honor the love you've shown me every day

I'm sorry mom and dad, for the mess I've made

Forgive me, guide me, in your love I'll fade.

82. Guiding Light

Oh, a teacher, a beacon of light
A second mother, in your highs and lows, shining bright
Always there for the holes, to mend and to guide
In the classroom of life, by your side
With wisdom and patience, they impart their knowledge
Nurturing minds, helping them flourish and acknowledge
The power of learning, the joy of discovery
A teacher's impact, profound and visionary
Through challenges and triumphs, they stand tall
Encouraging growth, inspiring all
In the journey of education, they play a vital role
Guiding hearts and minds, shaping the soul
So here's to the teachers, the unsung heroes
Who light the path, where knowledge flows
In their care and dedication, we find our way
Oh, a teacher, a guiding light, day by day.

83. Beyond the Trauma

A trauma, a wound so deep
One that cuts you to the core
It shakes your soul, makes it weep
But remember, it's not who you are
It may have left scars upon your skin
And pain that lingers in your heart
But know this, my dear kin
Your strength will never depart
For you are more than a memory
More than a single event
You're a resilient being
With unbreakable fortitude within
So hold your head up high
And stand tall against the tide
For though the trauma may not die
You'll overcome and thrive
It may try to define you
But you are stronger than its grasp
With courage and grace, you'll break through
And leave it in your past
Don't let it rob you of your light
Or take away your worth

You are a shining star
Even in the darkest of Earth
Let go of any shame or blame
Embrace yourself with love and care
For in spite of all that came
You rise above, fierce and rare
So dear one, never forget
A trauma does not define
The beautiful person that's been set
Within you, radiant and divine.

84. Unfolding Success

In chaos thrives a girl, untamed and wild,
Whose dreams soar high, relentless and unbound.
Amidst the whispers, doubts so loud,
She crafts her path, steadfast and proud.
They say her ways are but a messy maze,
A road to nowhere, a futile phase.
Yet she paints her world with colors bright,
Defying norms, embracing her light.
Through storms and doubts, she finds her grace,
In every stumble, a lesson to embrace.
For in her mess, a beauty unfurled,
A story of resilience, against a doubting world.
With every stride, she proves them wrong,
Her spirit fierce, her journey strong.
For success is not in perfection's mold,
But in the courage to be unapologetically bold.
So let them talk, let doubts fade away,
She'll rise above, come what may.
For in her heart, a fire burns bright,
A messy girl's journey, a radiant light.

85. Colours of Inspiration

In life's canvas, colors dance and play,
Each hue a story, in its own unique way,
Let's delve into the shades that pave the day,
And find motivation in their vibrant array.
Start with red, the fire of passion's ignite,
A bold reminder to chase dreams in sight,
With courage ablaze, embrace the fight,
And turn challenges into victories bright.
Orange speaks of warmth, like a sun-kissed glow,
Radiating energy, a relentless flow,
In its golden embrace, let ambitions grow,
And seize the day with a determined go.
Yellow, the joy of a new dawn's rise,
A beacon of hope, amid cloudy skies,
In its cheerful glow, let optimism rise,
And see opportunities through optimistic eyes.
Green whispers of growth, like nature's embrace,
A reminder to evolve, find your inner grace,
In its verdant arms, find your rightful place,
And bloom with wisdom, at your own pace.
Blue soothes the soul, like a tranquil sea,
A calm amidst storms, a serenity key,

And find inner peace, in moments free.
Purple, a regal hue, of dreams unfurled,
A realm of imagination, where visions swirl,
In its majestic glow, let ambitions twirl,
And paint your life's canvas with colors unfurl.
So, let colors inspire, in their radiant flight,
A palette of motivation, shining bright,
In life's intricate tapestry, weave with delight,
And embrace each shade, with all your might.

86. Galaxies of Illumination

Gaze upon the stars that twinkle, in the vast expanse above,
Each one a beacon of inspiration, filling hearts with love.
In their distant light, a message of hope and endless possibility,
Reminding us of our own potential, in every dream's reality.
Let the stars guide us through the night, with their celestial
grace,
Lighting pathways of discovery, in every new embrace.
or in their shimmering brilliance, a reminder we hold dear,
We're made of stardust and dreams, destined to persevere.

87. Mountains of Resolve

Like towering mountains standing tall, against the sky they rise,
Unyielding in their majesty, beneath the azure skies.
Each peak a testament to strength, each valley a trial faced,
Our resolve as solid as the rock, in challenges embraced.
Let the mountains inspire us, with their steadfast, resolute
stance,
For in their rugged beauty, we find courage to advance.
Like the mountains, firm in our resolve, we stand against the
tide,
With unwavering determination, our spirits cannot be denied.

88. Seeds of Strength

Deep within the fertile soil, where life begins anew,

Lie the seeds of inner strength, waiting to breakthrough.

With roots that delve deep, and branches that reach high,

We grow and flourish, beneath the boundless sky.

Nurture the seeds within your soul, with patience and with care,

For in their growth and blossoming, resilience blooms fair.

Like a garden of possibilities, each bloom a victory won,

The seeds of strength within us, shine bright beneath the sun.

89. Whispers of Wind

Listen to the whispers of the wind, a gentle, guiding voice,
Revealing secrets of endurance, in every gust's rejoice.
It dances freely through the air, with courage as its song,
Encouraging us to rise above, to where we truly belong.
Let the wind carry dreams aloft, on wings of hope and light,
In its whispers, find the courage to face the darkest night.
For in the softest breeze, a message clear and true,
Strength resides within us, waiting to breakthrough.

90. Rivers of Resilience

In the gentle flow of rivers, where currents bend and twist,
There lies a timeless lesson, in resilience firmly kissed.
Like water shaping stones, we mold our paths anew,
Adapting, persevering, in challenges we renew.
Through meandering journeys, in every ebb and flow,
Our strength shines through adversity, a steady, constant glow.
So let us flow like rivers, embracing change with grace,
For in resilience's embrace, we find our rightful place.

91. Unleashing Potential

In the whispers of the passing hours,
Where tasks pile high like blooming flowers,
A soul adrift in procrastination's tide,
Fearing the journey, where dreams reside.
But listen closely to the beating heart,
A rhythm of courage, ready to start,
For in each moment, a choice is made,
To conquer fears, to not evade.
Embrace the challenge, face the storm,
For within you lies a fire warm,
Ignite the passion, let it blaze,
Through doubts and worries, find your ways.
Procrastination, a fleeting shadow,
Cast aside, let determination grow,
With every step, you gain ground,
In perseverance, success is found.
So rise, oh soul, with purpose true,
Your dreams await, they're calling you,
In the midst of work, find your flow,
For greatness blooms where efforts grow.

92. Starbound Dreams

In the vast expanse of dreams untold,
Where aspirations shimmer bright and bold,
A whisper lingers in the night's embrace,
"Shoot for the moon, reach for that space."
For even if your aim may stray,
And the moon seems distant, far away,
Fear not the journey, fear not the miles,
For in the sky, the stars' warm smiles.
Each effort made, each step you take,
A constellation of hope, a dream awake,
No goal too lofty, no dream too grand,
In the universe, you'll find your stand.
So, shoot for the moon with all your might,
Let determination be your guiding light,
And if you miss, don't let hope fade,
Among the stars, your legacy is made.

93. Endless Endeavours

When one path ends, another begins,
A cycle of effort that never rescinds.
Each finish line marks a new start,
A chance to ignite the fire in your heart.
For every accomplishment, celebrate with glee,
Then set your sights on what's yet to be.
With each hurdle cleared and challenge met,
The next endeavor becomes your bet.
In the rhythm of life, this truth holds strong,
Keep moving forward, where you belong.
Embrace the journey, never stand still,
For with each finished effort, you gain the skill.
So let the quote inspire your soul,
To keep striving, to reach the goal.
With determination and unwavering grit,
Start another effort, never quit.

94. The Limitless Horizon

In the realm of dreams, where hope takes flight,
Tomorrow's canvas awaits, bathed in light.
But doubts of today, like shadows, loom,
Casting uncertainty, dimming the room.
Yet, within each doubt, a spark resides,
A flicker of courage, where faith abides.
For limits are but illusions we create,
When in our hearts, determination waits.
So let not doubts tether your soaring soul,
Embrace the unknown, let your dreams unfold.
For in the tapestry of time, doubts fade away,
And the boundless horizon of tomorrow's play.
Believe in the journey, the path you tread,
For the only limit is the one in your head.
Embrace the challenges, with courage and might,
And realize tomorrow, in its radiant light.

95. Flowing Time, Eternal Pursuit

Tick-tock, the clock whispers in rhyme,
A rhythm of moments, fleeting in time.
"Don't watch," it beckons, with steady beat,
"Do what I do, keep moving your feet."
Each second a whisper, a chance to embrace,
The dance of life, in its ever-changing pace.
For clocks may tick, and hours may pass,
But it's in the journey, we find meaning at last.
Keep going, dear heart, with unwavering stride,
Through valleys of challenges, and peaks of pride.
Let not the clock's ticking sow seeds of doubt,
But fuel your resolve, let courage sprout.
For time is a canvas, awaiting your art,
Each moment a stroke, from the depths of your heart.
So heed the clock's wisdom, in its rhythmic flow,
And with each tick, let your dreams grow.
Don't watch the clock, but let it inspire,
To live fully, with passion and fire.
For in the symphony of life, you play your part,
Don't just watch the clock; follow your heart.

96. Embrace your time

In the fleeting hours of life's fleeting span,
A reminder echoes, like grains of sand.
"Your time is limited," the whisper comes clear,
So don't lose yourself in another's sphere.
Each heartbeat counts, a rhythm divine,
A melody of moments, yours to define.
Don't trade your dreams for another's gaze,
Let passion guide you through life's maze.
For in the tapestry of existence, you hold the thread,
Crafting your story, where dreams are bred.
Don't be a shadow in someone else's light,
Embrace your uniqueness, let your spirit take flight.
The clock ticks on, with relentless might,
Each tick a reminder of life's finite sight.
So cherish each moment, in your own stride,
Don't waste your time living another's ride.
Let your heart lead, with courage unfurled,
For your time is precious, your own precious world.
Live authentically, in every breath you take,
For your life's journey is yours to make.